Regions of the United States: New England

Mark Stewart

Chicago, Illinois

© 2006 Raintree
Published by Raintree, a division of Reed Elsevier, Inc.
Chicago, Illinois

Customer Service 888-363-4266

Visit our website at www.heinemannraintree.com

Produced for Raintree by
White-Thomson Publishing Ltd.
Bridgewater Business Centre
210 High Street, Lewes, BN7 2NH

For information, address the publisher:
Raintree, 100 N. LaSalle, Suite 1200, Chicago, IL 60602

Edited by Susan Crean
Page layout by Malcolm Walker
Photo research by Amy Sparks
Illustrations by John Fleck

Printed in China by CTPS

11 10 09
10 9 8 7 6 5 4 3

ISBN 13: 978-1-4109-2306-6

Library of Congress
Cataloging-in-Publication Data

Stewart, Mark, 1960-
  New England / Mark Stewart.
    p. cm. -- (Regions of the USA)
  Includes bibliographical references and index.
  ISBN 1-4109-2306-1 (hc) -- ISBN 1-4109-2314-2 (pb)
  1. New England--Juvenile literature. I. Title. II. Series.
F4.3.S83 2007
974--dc22

                    2006004700

Acknowledgments
The publisher would like to thank the following for permission to reproduce photographs:
pp. 4, 15, 16A, 33, 39, 42, 48 Jeff Greenberg; pp. 5, 47 David Frazier; pp. 6A, 12, 13, 27A, 32B, 49, 51 Dean Abramson; p. 6B Brandon Clark/iStock; p. 8 Boyer/Roger-Viollet/Topfoto; p. 9 Library of Congress; p. 10 Todd Gipstein/Corbis; pp. 11, 26-27, 38, 50 The Image Works/Topfoto; p. 14A James L. Amos/Corbis; pp. 16-17 Craig Tuttle/Corbis; p. 18 Rick Friedman/Corbis; p. 19 Ted Horowitz/Corbis; p. 20 Jan Tyler/iStock; p. 21 Bruce MacQueen/iStock; pp. 22-23, 36 Gibson Stock Photography; p. 24 Kelly Newlin/DoD/CNP/Corbis; p. 25 Justin Horrocks/iStock; p. 28 Judy Griesedieck/Corbis; p. 29 Phil Schermeister/Corbis; pp. 30-31 James Marshall/Corbis; pp. 31A, 35 James P. Blair/Corbis; p. 32A Rob Sylvan/iStock; p. 34 Ed Halley/iStock; p. 37 Rick Friedman/Corbis; p. 40 Marc Serota/Reuters/Corbis; p. 41 Kevin Fleming/Corbis; p. 43 Greg Nicholas/iStock; p. 44 Mike Blake/Reuters/Corbis; p. 45A Duomo/Corbis; p. 45B Icon SMI/Corbis; p. 46 Lee Snider/Corbis.

Every effort has been made to contact copyright holders of any material reproduced in this book. Any omissions will be rectified in subsequent printings if notice is given to the publisher.

Cover photo of a farm in Vermont Water reproduced with permission of Bibikow/Viesti Associates

Contents

Some words are shown in bold, **like this**. You can find out what they mean by looking in the glossary.

New England

State names

Two New England state names are Native American. Connecticut comes from a word meaning "beside the long **tidal** river." Massachusetts, already in use when settlers arrived, means "at the great hill." Other state names in the region have European roots. New Hampshire comes from the county of Hampshire, England. Rhode island comes from the Greek island of Rhodes. Vermont comes from *vert mont*, French for "green mountain." Maine was a word used for the **mainland**.

There are many things that set New England apart from all other places in the United States. Different people would argue for different things when it comes to deciding what they like best about New England.

Campers might say the best thing about New England is the mysterious and beautiful north woods of Maine. Watersports lovers would argue for the Connecticut coastline. Snowboarders would vote for the snow-capped mountains of Vermont. Visitors to the New Hampshire countryside on a fall day would tell you that it is the smell of a crackling fire. Then there are the people who just can't leave the city. They might say that Boston is the best thing about New England.

The White Mountains of northern New Hampshire are a popular destination for hikers.

▼

Proud and independent

What is it about New England that makes people want to live there, or want to visit again and again? It is more than the crisp air, beautiful scenery, and small-town charm. It is more than the region's wonderful history and amazing legends. What makes New England special is that every street in every city and town seems to have its own "personality." New Englanders are fiercely independent. They are proud of the things that make them different—not just from each other, but from everyone else in the United States. This is sometimes called the "Yankee spirit."

Stowe, Vermont, is typical of the picture-perfect small towns found all around New England.

Find out later...

What famous sites in United States history can be found in the city of Boston?

What crop comes from this tree?

Which famous university is this?

▲
Summertime in New England draws people to its beaches, such as Wells Beach in Maine.

More to explore

The more you explore the New England states, the more interesting facts you learn. Did you know that Maine is the only state with a one-syllable name? Did you know that the Supreme Court building in Washington DC is made from Vermont **granite**? Did you know that Connecticut is home to the country's oldest newspaper, *The Hartford Courant*?

You are here

New England is located in the Northeast of the United States. It is made up of America's six easternmost states: Connecticut, Rhode Island, Massachusetts, Vermont, New Hampshire, and Maine. It covers an area of almost 63,000 square miles (163,170 square kilometers). Some important cities in the region include Boston in Massachusetts, Providence in Rhode Island, and Hartford and New Haven in Connecticut.

Around 14 million people live and work in New England year-round. The number of people in New England increases during the winter, thanks to its many ski slopes and hunting lodges. Even more people visit in the summer, vacationing on its lakes and beaches, or visiting its many small towns and historic sites.

Many of the people who work in—and visit—the city of Boston get there by commuter ferry.
▼

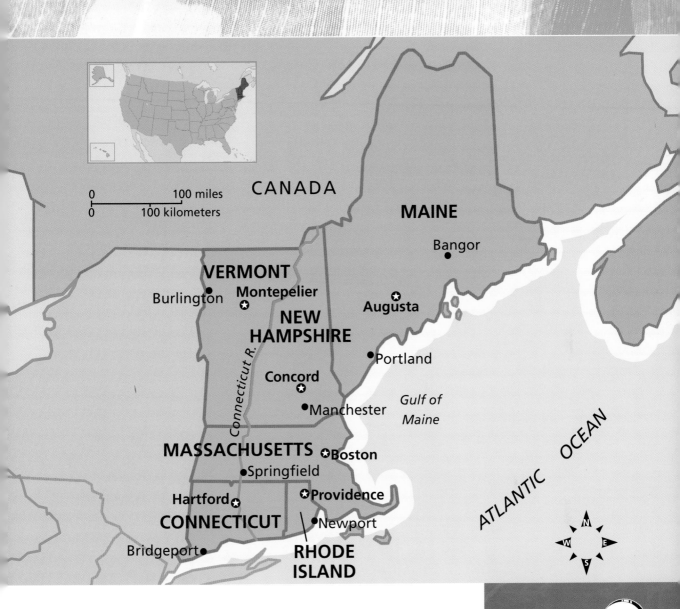

CANADA

MAINE

VERMONT
Burlington Montepelier
NEW
HAMPSHIRE
Augusta
Bangor
Portland
Gulf of
Maine
Concord
Manchester
MASSACHUSETTS Boston
Springfield
Hartford Providence
CONNECTICUT Newport
Bridgeport RHODE
ISLAND

Connecticut R.

ATLANTIC OCEAN

0   100 miles
0   100 kilometers

New England

The Northeastern region of the country is called New England because this is the part of the country where English people first settled in the United States in large numbers. Other parts of America were settled by people from other European countries, including the French, Spanish, and Dutch. Although the United States won its freedom from Great Britain more than 200 years ago, the people of this region are still proud to call themselves New Englanders.

Fact file

State	Population	Size
Connecticut	3,400,000	4,845 sq. mi. (12,869 sq. km)
Maine	1,300,000	30,869 sq. mi. (79,950 sq. km)
Massachusetts	6,400,000	7,840 sq. mi. (20,305 sq. km)
New Hampshire	1,200,000	8,968 sq. mi. (23,227 sq. km)
Rhode Island	1,100,000	1,045 sq. mi. (2,707 sq. km)
Vermont	621,000	9,250 sq. mi. (23,957 sq. km)

People and History

Native Americans were the first people to live in the land that is today New England. The Native Americans of New England included members of the Algonquin, Penobscot, Pennacook, Abnaki, Wampanoag, and Iroquois people. They lived in this region for many centuries.

The first Europeans to set foot in New England were explorers and fishers—some as early as 1,000 years ago. The first European settlers arrived in the 1600s. They lived alongside Native Americans until 1675, when the tribes of New England organized **resistance** to the settlers and war broke out. Over the next 100 years, the Native American **population** shrank as the number of settlers increased.

A vanishing people

New England's Native Americans suffered greatly after their uprising in 1675. After they were defeated by the colonists, many were rounded up and executed. Others were sold into slavery and sent to colonies in the Caribbean. Thousands more fled to New York and Canada. Only a few groups stayed in the region, living in small settlements in Connecticut, Massachusetts, and New Hampshire.

The Native Americans of New England were pushed out of the region as white settlers arrived.

Early settlers

People living in New England today can trace their roots to different countries and **cultures**. Many of their **ancestors** came to New England from Europe looking for the same thing: opportunity. The very first settlers in the region were mainly English and Dutch. They hoped to farm the region's rich soil and trade with Native Americans.

The first area settled in New England was eastern Massachusetts, where the Pilgrims landed in 1620. From there communities spread north into Maine and New Hampshire, and south into Connecticut. These were mostly English-speaking people, though some Dutch traders moved into Connecticut. Vermont was the last area to be settled, in the 1760s.

Fact file

Rhode Island colonists burned a British ship in 1772. This was the first action colonists took against British rule.

New England's early farmers had little contact with Europe. As a result they became very independent.

▼

A sense of independence

The first **colonists** who sailed to the **New World** believed they were coming to a land of opportunity. What they found, however, was a harsh and dangerous land. They felt very **isolated** from their homelands at first. Later, they began to develop a sense of **independence**. Not surprisingly, the people of New England were the first to start the fight for independence from Great Britain.

History comes alive

What was life in the Northeast like two centuries ago? There are many historic sites in New England that recreate this experience. One of the most popular is Mystic Seaport in Connecticut, a recreation of a coastal village from the 1800s.

A connection to the ocean

New England's long coastline and rich waters made it ideal for fishing, ocean trade, and shipbuilding. This connection to the ocean attracted people from Europe's **seafaring** cultures, including Portugal and Italy. Telephone directories in many coastal towns are still full of Portuguese and Italian names.

In the early days of New England, whaling was the most important business in the seaports of Connecticut, Maine and Massachusetts. The last wooden whaling boat in the world—the *Charles M. Morgan*—can be seen in Mystic, Connecticut. Today, the ports of New England are famous for their lobster. More than 70 million pounds (32 million kilograms) of lobster are caught each year by New England fishermen.

Visitors to Mystic Seaport can learn about how the ocean influenced the history of this region.
▼

Colonial New England

Life was not easy for the first settlers along New England's coasts and rivers. Every day was a fight for survival. Disease and starvation were always threatening. In time the settlers learned to farm, fish, and hunt, and trade with their Native American neighbors. This left time for people to build better homes and for those with special skills to open businesses. These settlements grew into villages and towns.

With more people living and working in New England, there was a need for a strong and fair government. After Connecticut became a colony, it wrote the Fundamental Orders of Connecticut, which called for a **legislature** and an elected governor. The writers of the United States Constitution used this document as a model a century later.

Touro **Synagogue**, America's oldest synagogue, was built in 1763 in Rhode Island.

▶

Fight for independence

By the 1770s, New Englanders were tired of British rule. In fact, New Hampshire declared its independence from Great Britain a month before the rest of the thirteen colonies. In 1775 the fight for independence began. The first shots of the American Revolution were fired in the Massachusetts towns of Lexington and Concord, outside of Boston.

Vermont, the country

While there is a common history in this region, each of the six states has its own history as well. For example, the territory that is now Vermont was claimed by both New Hampshire and New York. The people of Vermont settled this argument by declaring themselves an independent nation in 1777, until it became a state in 1791.

The green mountain boys

In the 1760s, a group of skilled woodsmen called the Green Mountain Boys was formed to protect Vermont. In the early days of the American Revolution, the Green Mountain Boys fought battles against the British and won. News of their victories gave the colonists hope in their fight for freedom.

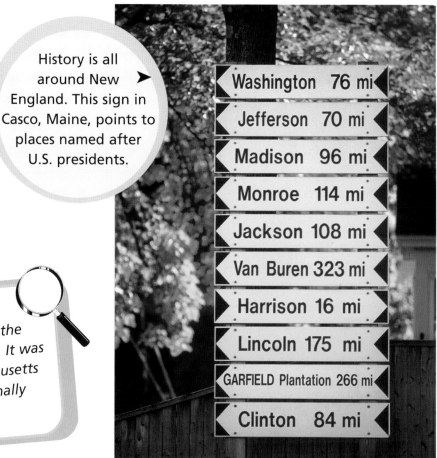

History is all around New England. This sign in Casco, Maine, points to places named after U.S. presidents.

Washington 76 mi
Jefferson 70 mi
Madison 96 mi
Monroe 114 mi
Jackson 108 mi
Van Buren 323 mi
Harrison 16 mi
Lincoln 175 mi
GARFIELD Plantation 266 mi
Clinton 84 mi

Fact file

Maine was not one of the original thirteen colonies. It was actually part of Massachusetts until 1820, when it finally became a state.

Industries and immigrants

The strong, swift rivers in this region provided power for America's first factories. The nation's first **textile** mill, for example, was built in Pawtucket, Rhode Island, in 1790. During the 1800s, New England became the most important **manufacturing** area in the United States. **Immigrants** from poor countries in Europe, such as Ireland, flooded into the region. Steady work later attracted people from Poland, Hungary, and Russia.

In recent years, opportunity has brought many **Latino** and Asian people to New England. In a way, they are chasing the same dream the first settlers did. The promise of jobs in the **service industry** and manufacturing, and a chance for a good education, create thousands of "new" New Englanders each year.

The enormous Topham Mill in Maine is a reminder of New England's history as a center of the textile industry.

▼

French speakers

After America won its independence from Great Britain in 1783, many thousands of English **subjects** moved north to Canada. Some of Canada's French-speaking population decided to move down into Maine and New Hampshire. French is still spoken in parts of northern Maine, where you can still see road signs in French.

13

Land in the Area

New England has three very different **landscapes**: coastal, river valleys, and mountains. As you might guess, the **climate** in these regions can be very different. The higher you go, the cooler it gets; the closer to the coast you are, the milder the weather.

The seashore along the Long Island **Sound** and Atlantic Ocean is made up of bustling port cities and quaint communities with breathtaking views. Block Island, Martha's Vineyard, Nantucket, the Cape Cod beaches, and the islands off the coast of Maine are some of the most scenic places in North America.

The peaceful inlets of the Long Island Sound make the Connecticut coastline a popular place to live.

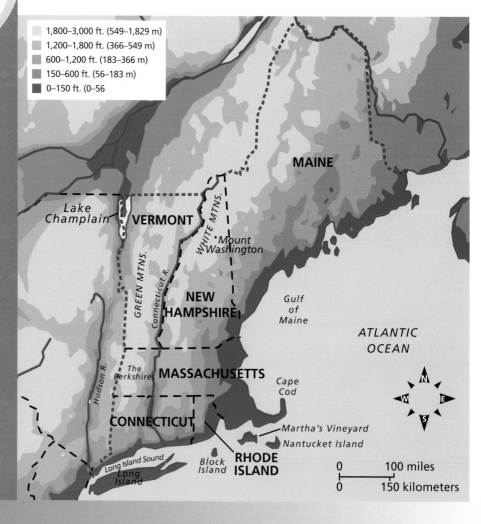

1,800–3,000 ft. (549–1,829 m)
1,200–1,800 ft. (366–549 m)
600–1,200 ft. (183–366 m)
150–600 ft. (56–183 m)
0–150 ft. (0–56

MAINE

Lake Champlain VERMONT

WHITE MTNS.

•Mount Washington

GREEN MTNS.

Connecticut R.

NEW HAMPSHIRE

Gulf of Maine

ATLANTIC OCEAN

Hudson R.

The Berkshires MASSACHUSETTS

Cape Cod

CONNECTICUT

Martha's Vineyard
Nantucket Island

Long Island Sound
Long Island

Block Island

RHODE ISLAND

0   100 miles
0   150 kilometers

N
W E
S

Mountains

The region's mountains include the Berkshires, Green Mountains, and White Mountains. They cut diagonally from western Massachusetts up through Maine to the Canadian **border**. They include the northern end of the Appalachian Mountains in the United States.

Water comes from the melting snow on the heavily forested mountains of New Hampshire and Vermont. It then flows down through Massachusetts and Connecticut and creates river valleys.

Nice view

Cadillac Mountain, on Mount Desert Island in Maine, is the highest point on America's Atlantic coast. It stands 1,530 feet (466 meters) tall. The highest point in the region is Mount Washington, in New Hampshire, at 6,288 feet (1,916 meters). Mount Washington is one of five peaks in the White Mountains named after presidents. The others are Adams, Jefferson, Madison, and Monroe.

The gently sloping mountains of Maine are very popular with hikers, campers, and mountain bikers.

Water features

The Atlantic coastline is important to most states in New England. Connecticut, for instance, has 90 miles (145 kilometers) of calm coastline known as the Long Island Sound. Maine's coastline is 228 miles (367 kilometers) long, but it is rough and rocky. The state is also well known for its 5,000 rivers and streams.

Water also plays an important role in two other states: Rhode Island and Massachusetts. Much of life in Rhode Island takes place on the islands and along the waterways that make up Narragansett Bay. Port cities in Massachusetts, such as Boston, Gloucester, and New Bedford, are important to the state's **economy**.

Every summer, the beaches of Cape Cod come alive. Vacationers enjoy swimming, fishing, and a number of other activities.

Cape Cod

The Massachusetts coast is more than 300 miles (483 kilometers) long, but it can be summed up in two words: Cape Cod. This 65-mile (105-kilometer) stretch of Atlantic coastline is one of the most famous and popular in the world. The Cape Cod National Seashore is a national park that includes six swimming beaches, eleven nature trails, and a variety of picnic areas and scenic overlooks.

Mountains and forests

Vermont is a state of mountains. The Green Mountains, part of the Appalachian chain, run right up the center of the state. There are 80 peaks above 3,000 feet (914 meters) in Vermont. New Hampshire is best known for one particular mountain—Mount Washington. At 6,288 feet (1,916 meters) it is the region's tallest peak, and also one of the windiest spots in the United States.

Maine, on the other hand, is a land of forests. Forests cover more than 90 percent of the state—the most in the region. New Hampshire has the second highest forest coverage in New England, with 85 percent.

New Hampshire's Mount Washington, the region's tallest peak, ▲ is part of the White Mountains.

Written in stone

New England may not be known for its mineral deposits, but **garnet** and granite are important products for the region. A huge deposit of garnet in southwestern Maine has made the state one of the country's largest producers of this gemstone. The variety of colors and patterns in New Hampshire's granite makes it an important source for builders and designers, and also gives New Hampshire its nickname: The Granite State.

New England's climate

When you see pictures of snow-covered mountains and sun-tanned swimmers, it is easy to believe that New England is a region of "extremes." In fact, the weather is mostly extreme in mountainous areas and in northern areas, where it can get very cold in the winter. The overall climate in the rest of New England can be quite mild, especially in the south.

The average temperature in New England during the summer is around 70 °F (21 °C), but summer heat waves often bring temperatures into the 90s °F (30s °C). Even when the days are hot, the evenings usually are cool and comfortable.

Rain and snow

New England receives 40 to 50 inches (102 to 127 centimeters) of rain each year. In the winter more than ten feet (three meters) of snow falls on some areas. The heaviest snow occurs in the Berkshire Mountains of Massachusetts, the Green Mountains of Vermont, and the White Mountains of New Hampshire.

The lovely dunes and long beaches of Martha's Vineyard make it a favorite of summer vacationers.

Winter weather

The average winter temperature near the Atlantic coast is between 20 and 30 °F (-7 and -1 °C). In Vermont, and in the northern parts of New Hampshire and Maine, the average winter temperature drops into the teens.

Winter cold spells are common, especially inland, where the thermometer often dips below zero. On these days, some people bundle up and stay close to a heat source. Others grab their skis and snowboards, anxious to work up a sweat on the slopes.

Many New Englanders believe their region is prettiest after a winter snowfall.

Big wind

On April 12, 1934, a wind gust of 231 miles (372 kilometers) per hour was recorded atop Mt. Washington in New Hampshire. This is still the strongest wind ever recorded on earth. In 1997 a typhoon in Guam came close to breaking the record.

Fact file

In 1876 a freak snowstorm hit New England on the Fourth of July!

19

Animals and Plants

Just passing through

Cape Cod is home to more than 250 species of birds. Many, however, are just visitors—on their way north for the summer or south for the winter. In this bird-watcher's paradise, types of **migrating** birds range from familiar sandpipers to rare petrels and grebes.

New England is home to some of America's most familiar animals. Raccoons, porcupines, gray squirrels, and crows are perfectly suited to every part of the region. As more people moved to the Northeast, these animals quickly **adapted** to the changes in human population.

Some animals were not so lucky. Overhunting and loss of **habitat** threatened many kinds of animals after settlers arrived. In recent years, however, there have been many amazing "comebacks." This happened naturally in some cases. In other cases, species were re-introduced and "managed" until their populations grew large enough so they could survive.

Large flocks of snow geese are among the many migrating bird species that pass through New England.

Back again

Black bear, white-tailed deer, and beaver are all thriving in areas where they were once threatened. Bird species that are growing once again in New England include bald eagles, great blue herons, ospreys, and pileated woodpeckers.

Moose have also made a comeback. The best place to see them is around the ponds and lakes of Maine's Baxter State Park. They make their way to the water at sunrise and sunset each day.

Newcomers

Over the past 100 years, a handful of new animals have found the Northeast to their liking. They have expanded their ranges and now are full-time residents. These species include the coyote and turkey vulture.

Aquariums

Two of the most popular places to view New England's marine life are the New England Aquarium in Boston and the Mystic Marinelife Aquarium, in Mystic, Connecticut. These modern aquariums recreate the natural habitats of the coastlines, rivers, and lakes of the Northeast.

Two does forage for food in the snow. The white-tailed deer is one of New England's many ▲ year-round residents.

21

The pine tree

The pine tree has been a symbol for New England for many centuries. Long before settlers arrived, one of the most powerful tribes in the region was the Penacook. This is an Algonquin word meaning "children of the pine tree." Once settlers arrived in the 1620s, the colony at Plymouth, Massachusetts, created a seal that featured two pine trees. The flag of New England from the 1680s to the 1770s also featured a pine tree.

A land of tall trees

The trees in New England include different species of pine, ash, maple, beech, hemlock, spruce, poplar, oak, cherry, and sycamore. Tree lovers like to go to the Mohawk Trail State Forest, in the Berkshire Mountains of western Massachusetts. This is where some of the tallest trees in the region grow.

Numerous plants and trees thrive in New England's river valleys such as those found in the Berkshire Mountains.

▼

22

Plants of New England

The plants and trees of New England may be the most studied and understood on earth. Scientists have been watching the plants of this region for almost 400 years. More than 4,000 different types of plants can be found in the six states, along with more than 250 types of trees, shrubs, vines, and woody plants.

Around half of these plants and trees can be found within an hour of where Vermont, New Hampshire, and Massachusetts meet. This is because the landscape and climate varies dramatically in this area.

Cathedral Pines

For many years the Cathedral Pines **Preserve** of Cornwall, Connecticut was one of the most amazing places in the region. Its white pine trees stood here for hundreds of years. Many of these trees soared to more than 150 feet (46 meters). Sadly, in 1989, a severe storm toppled many of these majestic trees.

Cities and Towns

Megalopolis

The towns and cities between the New York-Connecticut border and the Boston metropolitan area have become very popular places to live. Over the last 50 years, they have actually grown together in many places, and now look like one long, community, stretching across much of the Northeast. This is called a **megalopolis**.

The largest city in the Northeast region is Boston, Massachusetts. Its population is around 600,000. This may be small by big-city standards, but there are six million people living in the Boston **metropolitan area**. The city itself is small enough to walk almost anywhere.

The Freedom Trail, which takes visitors past many of the city's historic places, is only three miles (five kilometers) long. For those who prefer to ride, Boston has a great rail system called the T. There are also tours on vehicles that can travel on both land and water called duck boats.

History is never far away in New England. Here the famous USS *Constitution* sails through Boston Harbor.

Famous sites

Among the most popular areas in the city is the Boston Common and Public Gardens. The Common is America's oldest public park, dating back to the 1600s. Other sights include America's most famous ship, the USS *Constitution*, the Museum of Science, the Old North Church, Paul Revere's house, Newberry Street, and Boston's oldest neighborhood, the North End.

Boston, a stop for escaped slaves on the **Underground Railroad** in the 1800s, is also home to the African Meeting House, the first church in the United States built by free African Americans, and the Black Heritage Trail, which traces the route many escaped slaves took through the city.

The city of Boston may be crowded, but it still has plenty of green space, including the nation's oldest park.
▼

Higher learning

Across the Charles River from Boston, in Cambridge, Massachusetts, are two of America's most famous centers of learning, Harvard University and the Massachusetts Institute of Technology (MIT). Harvard is more than 360 years old and is known for its schools of business, medicine, and law. MIT dates back to 1916 and has become the country's most important school of engineering science.

Springfield

The city of Springfield, Massachusetts, attracts tourists with a wide variety of interests. It is home to the Naismith Memorial Basketball Hall of Fame, Springfield Armory (with its important weapons exhibit), and "Museum Quadrangle," where the region's science, art, and history come alive.

Industrial centers

The smaller cities of the Northeast region include Portland in Maine, Portsmouth in New Hampshire, Providence in Rhode Island, Springfield in Massachusetts, and Hartford and New Haven in Connecticut. These cities were important industrial centers in the 1800s and early 1900s. After years of decline, each has learned how to change with the times. Today, tourism makes up an important part of the business they do.

Architecture from three different centuries makes up the skyline of Providence, Rhode Island.

City life

Visitors to Portland, Maine's largest city, enjoy its waterside, art museums, and historic buildings. Its most famous structure is the Portland Head Light, a lighthouse commissioned by George Washington. Portsmouth is home to Strawberry Banke, a colonial seaport village.

Providence is known for its superb restaurants and a marvelous restored waterfront district. It is also home to the Rhode Island School of Design and its famous art museum.

The Portland Head Light in Maine was built in the late 1700s.

Hartford

Hartford, Connecticut, was the home of three famous American writers. Visitors can tour the Mark Twain Mansion and the homes of Noah Webster and Harriet Beecher Stowe. During the 1850s, Stowe wrote *Uncle Tom's Cabin*, a book that fanned the flames of the anti-slavery movement.

Small town life

New England has never lost its small-town flavor, even though some of the towns that were once small have become quite large. Some have grown because people have purchased second homes. Others are now considered suburbs of big cities.

Many small towns have grown because they have learned how to attract more tourists, such as the Massachusetts towns of Plymouth and Salem. Plymouth's "Plimoth Plantation" is a Pilgrim village from 1627 that is visited by more people than ever. Salem has created many attractions around its famous witch trials. These towns have become larger and more sophisticated because of this popularity.

Looking presidential

The towns of Kennebunk and Kennebunkport on Maine's southern coast were a well-kept secret until George H.W. Bush was elected president in 1988. His summer home on Walker's Point was in the news every time he took a break from the White House. "Bush-watchers" who decided to visit the area soon realized why the Bushes loved it here—it is home to some of the state's most beautiful and historic architecture.

Sea kayakers hope for a glimpse of former President George H.W. Bush near his home in Kennebunkport, Maine.

Hidden gems

Millinocket in Maine and Jaffrey in New Hampshire are two small towns in New England. Millinocket is near remote Baxter State Park and the Penobscot River. It is a favorite of whitewater paddlers. Jaffrey is close to Boston, yet it seems a million miles away. Serious hikers may visit Jaffrey on their way to Mt. Monadnock, which offers a challenging climb and amazing views.

Throughout the region, there are small towns that will always be small—and they like it that way. Tucked away in the forests of northern New England, they are among the quietest and most remote places in the region.

The area around Jaffrey, New Hampshire, offers the kind of peace and quiet that many people seek when they move to New England.

Commuterville

The towns of southwestern Connecticut serve as a suburb of New York City. Every morning, tens of thousands of commuters jump into their cars or hop on trains to get into the city. In recent years, many of these towns, including Greenwich, Darien, New Canaan, Stamford, and Ridgefield, have become large enough to attract "city" businesses. Now, people commute into these cities as much as they commute from them.

Rural Life

Farming and insurance

In the 1700s the tobacco farmers of Connecticut faced disaster every time they loaded a ship bound for England. If it sank in a storm or was captured by pirates, they would be ruined. The growers decided to pool their money and spread their risk out so each would be "insured" against a total loss. This was how the American insurance industry began.

Although the people who first settled the Northeast region were mostly farmers, the region itself does not have a lot of farmable land. This is one reason why many people headed west after arriving in North America.

The soil is rocky in eastern Massachusetts and much of Maine. In New Hampshire and Vermont, the land is too rugged and the valleys too narrow for major farming operations.

Despite its many river valleys, farming has always been a great challenge to the people of New England.
▼

Specialty farms

Despite there being little farmable land, there are small farms in New England. In Maine, hundreds of farms supply the country with potatoes. In Vermont and New Hampshire, small dairy farms still dot the landscape. Many are now producing rare cheeses and other specialty food items.

In the river valleys of Massachusetts and Connecticut, the soil is ideal for producing the nursery plants demanded by homeowners in the suburbs and landscape designers in the cities. Chickens do well in these areas, too. Eggs are one of Connecticut's most important agricultural products.

▲ The fall harvest in New England is a time of brilliant colors and pumpkin patches.

Haymakers

One of Connecticut's biggest crops is feed for horses. This includes hay and other plants grown for horses to eat. The state has more "leisure" horse-owners than any other state in the country, so it makes sense to grow their food nearby.

31

Maple syrup

The Northeast region's most famous crop is maple syrup. Most people think of Vermont when they think of syrup, but the truth is that it is made throughout the region, and north into Canada.

The best time to watch maple syrup being produced is at the end of winter, when the temperature rises and falls around the freezing point each day. This gets the sap flowing, and the "sugaring" process begins. The sap is collected and the syrup is finished when the water in the sap is boiled off.

Making syrup

Maple syrup just doesn't seem to taste as good unless it's collected the old-fashioned way. Most syrup makers still hammer spouts into the sugar maples and let the sap drip into buckets (above). More and more, however, syrup makers are drilling hundreds of holes into their trees and running the sap into collection vats through plastic tubing.

The lumber business is an important part of the economy in the northern part of New England.
▼

Working outside the cities

Much of New England's rural life has little to do with traditional farming. In Vermont, New Hampshire, and Maine, the crop that is harvested is trees. Thousands of people work as loggers, and thousands more work for businesses that turn the wood they produce into everything from lumber to paper to furniture.

Many people who live in rural areas now work in small offices and factories, in service industries such as tourism and real estate, or in the home-building business.

Goat grooming is part of the fun at an agricultural fair held in Maine.

▼

County Fairs take place throughout New England. Brooklyn, Connecticut, has held the Brooklyn Fair every year since 1851, which is a record for agricultural fairs in the United States. Each August, Brooklyn's population goes from 6,500 to more than 100,000 during the four-day event.

Getting Around

Railways old and new

In the days before automobiles were common, New England boasted one of the nation's most elaborate railroad systems. One of the most popular train lines—The Downeaster—was recently reopened. It connects Boston and Portland, Maine, on tracks that offer breathtaking water views.

New England is one of the easiest regions to move within. Major highways crisscross Connecticut, Massachusetts, and the Vermont-New Hampshire border. One of America's busiest interstates is I-95. It winds its way up the coast of New England.

Boston, a harbor city, has bridges, tunnels, and ferries to move people in and out. The Boston subway system moves people around the city. It is one of the nation's biggest and best, and also its oldest. Boston is also home to the region's largest airport, Logan International.

A system of modern highways moves people and products throughout the New England region.

Fact file
In 1901 Connecticut became the first state in the nation to post speed limits for automobiles.

A big dig

Boston is a very old city with narrow streets that run up, down, and around a steep hill. Driving from one part of the city to another can take a very long time, and traffic jams have been a problem for many years. In 1991 Boston began construction on the Central Artery and Tunnel project. The idea was to place the city's main highways underground to relieve traffic. In 2005 the "Big Dig" was done. Cars now travel quickly on an underground highway beneath the city. It was the largest urban project in American history.

Lake Champlain forms much of New England's western border. The state of New York is across the lake.

Lake Champlain

Much of the border between Vermont and New York State is formed by Lake Champlain. In the 1700s, this was the region's key north-south waterway. During the American Revolution, many important battles were fought over this important body of water.

Work in the Area

Hunting and fishing

One of the most important industries in Maine is hunting. Thousands of hunters head for the state's north woods each year to bag a trophy deer or moose. They spend millions of dollars in Maine's hunting lodges, hotels, sporting goods stores, and restaurants. Maine's streams and rivers also attract thousands of fishing enthusiasts.

The lives of working people have changed dramatically in New England over the past 50 years. Many of the industries that made this region America's most powerful were based on the energy supplied by rivers or on the region's many seaports.

As these became less important, a lot of businesses failed. The textile and leatherworking businesses were almost wiped out. Industries such as whaling disappeared completely.

The textile and leather industries employed thousands of people in the region during the 1800s. This old mill is now a museum.

▼

Tourism in New England

Manufacturing jobs have largely been replaced by jobs in service industries. The most important industry in New England today is tourism. Millions of people visit the region each year.

There is something for everyone in the Northeast, including skiing, swimming, hunting, fishing, hiking, biking, and boating. Making sure tourists have fun and plan a return visit is an important job.

The resort island of Martha's Vineyard, Maine, is a popular destination for tourists.

▼

Jewelry making

Rhode Island may be famous for summer resorts like Newport and Block Island, but two of its most important year-round industries are jewelry and silverware. These businesses have existed in the state since the 1800s. Unlike many older industries, they have been able to change with the times and stay ahead of foreign competition.

Businesses old and new

Although much of the industry that existed in the early days of New England has changed, many "traditional" businesses are still going strong. Hartford, Connecticut, for example, is still an important center for the insurance business. Boston, Massachusetts, remains a powerful city in banking and international trade.

The universities of New England are an important part of the economy, too. Besides educating future leaders, they are making huge contributions to society through scientific research. Many breakthroughs in medicine, computers, and **telecommunications** have come from this part of the United States.

Big bang!

For more than 200 years, New England has been a center for military goods, from cannons and rifles all the way to **nuclear submarines**. The Springfield rifle and Colt revolver were invented in this region. Today, tourists can actually visit the USS *Nautilus*, the first nuclear submarine, in Groton, Connecticut. This connection between New England and the military continues to provide jobs for thousands in the region.

Students relax at Yale University. Many of the nation's business and political leaders graduated from this school.

Gifts from the ocean

One industry that is as important today as it was 100 years ago is the harvesting of shellfish. Maine is famous for its lobsters and Connecticut is a center of oyster farming. Massachusetts and Rhode Island also have thriving shellfish industries.

Much of the seafood that reaches the nation's dinner tables—including cod, swordfish, and tuna—comes from the fishing ports of New England. Fishing has been a major business in the Northeast for hundreds of years. European fleets fished these same waters in the 1400s, many years before Christopher Columbus discovered America in 1492. In fact some believe that cod fisherman may have been the first to see the New England coastline.

A lobster trapper sizes up his catch. The ocean provides many jobs for the people of New England. ➤

Overfishing

Unfortunately, many of New England's traditional fishing grounds have been overfished. The industry is working with scientists to reverse this trend. For example, the region's lobster fishers throw back egg-laying females to ensure that there will be a good catch in future years.

Fact file

A few generations ago, lobster was so plentiful that a family had to work much harder to put a chicken on its table than a lobster. Today, the opposite is true.

Free Time

Popular theater

The Yale Repertory Theater and Long Wharf Theater, both in New Haven, Connecticut, and the Theater by the Sea in Providence, Rhode Island, draw some of the world's best creative talent. Many important plays have been performed here for the very first time. Many of the actors you see on television and in the movies used these (and other) New England theaters as stepping-stones to fame.

New England has been an important center of art and culture for more than 100 years. Music and dance lovers have much to choose from, from the Boston Symphony to the Boston Ballet Company to the nightclubs and concert halls that draw the region's many college students.

Among the region's most popular events are performances by the Boston Pops. This orchestra features classical musicians performing popular music. This tradition dates back to 1885. In 1929 the Boston Pops began its series of free concerts along the Charles River.

Bono of the band U2 sings along with the Boston Pops.

Museums

Museums are plentiful in the region. They include the world-renowned Museum of Fine Arts in Boston, Providence's Wheeler Gallery, the Museum of Art at the Rhode Island School of Design, and New Haven's Center of British Art.

Some of the region's best smaller museums are the Museum of American Art in New Britain, Connecticut, the Norman Rockwell Museum in Sturbridge, Massachusetts, and the Peabody Museum in Salem, Massachusetts.

The John F. Kennedy Library and Museum in Boston is one of the region's most famous buildings. ▼

Creative community

For more than 100 years, creative people have been drawn to the peace and beauty of New England's wild areas. There is plenty of privacy for those who want it. There are also places like the MacDowell Colony, a literary and artistic community in New Hampshire. Writers, poets, painters, and sculptors live together there. They share their ideas and give one another inspiration.

Fact file

Noah Webster of Connecticut published the first edition of his dictionary of the American language in 1806.

41

Food in New England

The favorite foods of New England come from the nearby ocean. Cod and lobster are the most popular types of seafood. Thanks to the different ethnic groups in the region—including people from Asia, the Mediterranean, and South America—these can be prepared in many different ways.

Wild game and local vegetables also find their way to the table in many restaurants. In general, the dishes of the Northeast are rich, heavy, and hearty.

What's cooking

Food festivals are big business in New England, especially along the shore. One of the best is the Taste of Block Island Seafood Festival and Chowder Cook-Off, in Rhode Island. Another is the "Lobsterfest" in Rockland, Maine. Rockland calls itself the "lobster capital of the world."

Seafood lovers can choose from dozens of festivals held each summer in New England.

Boston specialties

The region's most famous dishes all have "Boston" in their names. Boston clam chowder, a delicious clam and potato soup, is served all over the world. Boston cream pie is a marriage of rich whipped cream and chocolate. Sweet, savory Boston baked beans are so famous that Boston is nicknamed "Beantown." In the 1800s, the city's baseball team was actually named the Beaneaters!

Every evening, Boston's oldest neighborhood, the North End, comes alive with the smells of the city's most mouthwatering meals. The aromas from restaurants and apartment kitchens waft down the narrow streets, blending together a dozen different cultures and cooking styles. Some of the recipes are centuries old, with roots going back to the Mediterranean, Southeast Asia, South and Central America, and West Africa.

Big chill

One of the most popular food stops in New England is the Ben & Jerry's ice cream factory in Waterbury, Vermont. Here visitors can watch how ice cream goes from the cow to the container, and sample their favorite flavors at the end of a fun tour. Ben & Jerry's chose to build its factory in Vermont because of the region's strong dairy business and clean environment.

New England cooking offers many specialties, including famous Boston baked beans—sometimes served with barbecued ribs.

Sports

There are four big-league sports teams in New England: the Boston Red Sox (baseball), Boston Celtics (basketball), Boston Bruins (hockey), and New England Patriots (football). Rooting for these teams is a passion that unites the entire region.

Red Sox fans used to believe their team was cursed. After winning the World Series in 1918, they came close many times but never won it again. In 2004 the team finally "reversed the curse," and won it again.

The Boston Marathon

The region's most famous sports event is the Boston Marathon. It is a 26-mile (42-kilometer) race held each year on Patriot's Day. Patriot's Day is a holiday held on the third Monday in April each year in Maine and Massachusetts. The Boston Marathon was first held in 1897. The best runners make it to the finish line in just over two hours.

Richard Seymour carries his son and the championship trophy after the New England Patriots won the Super Bowl in 2005.

The Green Monster

Red Sox fans have nicknamed the left-field wall in Fenway Park the "Green Monster." The wall is more than 35 feet (11 meters) high, which makes it the tallest fence in baseball. There used to be a net atop the Green Monster to catch home runs. Now fans catch home runs in a special section of seats at the top of the wall.

Winter wonderland

When the snow falls on New England, the time is right for winter sports. Skiing, sledding, ice skating, and snowshoeing are all popular sports in the winter. Vermont is a popular destination for skiing, but there are more than 65 ski areas across all the New England states.

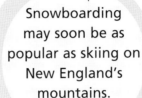

Snowboarding may soon be as popular as skiing on New England's mountains.

All downhill from here

Each winter, the world's top snowboarders gather atop Stratton Mountain in Vermont for the U.S. Open Snowboarding Championships. One of the highlights of this competition is the Junior Halfpipe, when kids 15 and under get to show their stuff.

Baseball fans enjoy a game at Boston's Fenway Park. The Green Monster towers above left field.

Recreation in New England

Picking the best way to have fun in New England can be hard work. There are so many places to go and things to see. Vermont is known for its skiing, but during the warm months its 765 state parks and forests draw many people.

New Hampshire's Mt. Washington, one of the harshest places on earth in winter, is mild the rest of the year. Visitors can ride an 1866 **cog railroad** to the peak, which soars more than a mile (1.6 kilometers) high. The views from Mt. Cadillac in Maine's Acadia National Park on Mount Desert Island are not as high, but the views of the Atlantic Ocean and Maine coastline are unlike any in America.

The Old Man is no more

One of the most popular stops for vacationers in the region used to be the Old Man of the Mountain. This rock formation towered over Profile Lake in New Hampshire's White Mountains. A few years ago, after standing watch for 200 million years, the Old Man's face broke away and tumbled down the mountain.

Mount Washington's famous cog railroad chugs up the tracks. It has been running for almost 150 years. ▶

46

Sightseeing

There is plenty to see and do in each of New England's six states. In Essex, Connecticut, you can take a seat on the Valley Railroad Steam Train. The classic locomotive chugs along an eight-mile track and stops at a ferry, which takes visitors to a castle. Visitors to Newport, Rhode Island, can explore old mansions and enjoy fine restaurants or just sit back and watch the sailboat races.

Other New Englanders spend their free time (and money) in the Indian-owned casinos in Connecticut. Children are not allowed in the casinos, but there are other attractions nearby, including the magnificent Mashantucket Pequot Museum and Research Center, which celebrates the heritage of the Pequot Indians.

Boston's Quincy Market and Faneuil Hall is one of New England's most popular sight-seeing stops.

The coast and a carousel

One of the best places in the region to relax is the Rhode Island coast. Here you will find the Roger Williams Park & Zoo—considered the best in New England—and America's oldest merry-go-round, the Flying Horse Carousel. It opened in 1867, and each horse is carved from a single piece of wood.

Festivals and fairs

Between the months of May and October, there are dozens of small festivals and fairs in New England every week. Some are strictly local, but others draw people from all over. The most famous is the Eastern States Exhibition in Springfield, Massachusetts. Everyone calls it the "Big E." It is one of the largest fairs in the United States, and it brings together young people who are interested in farming, crafts, and technology.

Stratton Mountain in Vermont brings together people from the creative community during the month-long Stratton Arts Festival. It is held every year from mid-September through mid-October. It features music, theater, dance, painting, and sculpture. When this event is over, the mountain is transformed into a world-class ski and snowboard resort.

Maine attractions

The historic resort town of Bar Harbor, Maine, is located on Mount Desert island. It plays host to festivals, concerts, and other events all summer long. For those who love old lighthouses, Maine offers the West Quoddy Head Lighthouse. President Thomas Jefferson had it built in 1808. Nearby is Sail Rock, the easternmost point in the United States.

The streets of Bar Harbor, Maine, host thousands of tourists each year.

Patriot's Day

Patriot's Day, which occurs on the third Monday of April, is celebrated throughout New England. Government workers and students in Massachusetts and Maine get the day off to honor the men and women who risked everything to win their freedom from the British in the 1700s.

Hill of a holiday

The students and workers of Boston get another day off in the spring. June 17, Bunker Hill Day, is a legal holiday in Boston. The holiday commemorates the battle of Bunker Hill that was fought during the American Revolution.

Something old

The Brimfield Antique Show, held in an open field three times a year in Brimfield, Massachusetts, is the most famous in the United States. People in the region are very serious about their antiques.

Entertainment is a big part of local fairs such as the Fryeburg Fair held in Maine each year.
▼

49

An Amazing Region

Ancient wonder

One of the greatest mysteries of New England can be found in the woods near Salem, New Hampshire. It is a large stone structure that seems to be aligned with the sun and the moon, and it is more than 4,000 years old. Little is known about the ancient people who used this site.

You could devote your entire life to exploring New England and not see everything. No matter how many towns you visit, summits you climb, or wild places you explore, there is always more to do. New England offers everything from colonial history to extreme sports, remote campsites to big cities, and mountain hideaways to long, sandy beaches.

For the people who live in the region, the possibilities for adventure change with the seasons. For those who travel to New England, each season offers something different wherever they go.

One popular way to explore New England is by kayak.

▼

New Englanders today

The people of New England are proud of the world they have made for themselves. Their sense of independence is as fierce as it was when they struck America's first blows for freedom. They have embraced modern life while keeping many of their old traditions.

The first settlers to arrive in New England were searching for opportunity and a better life for their families. They carved out a new home, and in time, a new nation. Today, many of the region's people are new to America. Yet they share many of the same goals with the first New Englanders who arrived almost 400 years ago.

Stephen King

One of New England's most famous writers is Stephen King. King was born in Portland, Maine. He writes horror, fantasy, and science fiction stories. King was one of the first authors to publish an "e-book" that could be downloaded from the Internet. Some of the scariest movies ever made were inspired by his books. Many of King's stories take place in New England.

The sun sets in Camden, a harbor town in Maine.
▼

51

Find Out More

Books to read

Cherry, Lynne. *A River Ran Wild: An Environmental History*. San Diego, CA: Harcourt Children's Books, 2002.

Fifer, Barbara. *EveryDay Geography of the United States*. New York, NY: Black Dog & Leventhal, 2000.

Ortakales, Denise. *The Legend Of The Old Man Of The Mountain*. San Diego, CA: Sleeping Bear Press, 2004.

Orr, Tamra B. *Salem Witch Trials*. Farmington Hills, MI: Blackbirch Press, 2003.

Vanderwarker, Peter. *Big Dig: Reshaping an American City*. Boston, MA: Little, Brown & Company, 2001.

Watters, David and Burt Feintuch. *The Encyclopedia of New England*. New Haven, CT: Yale University Press, 2005.

Places to visit

Ben & Jerry's (Waterbury, Vermont)
This ice cream factory offers tours that end with a delicious treat.

The Freedom Trail (Boston, Massachusetts)
This trail is a walking tour of sixteen sites and structures of historic importance.

Mount Washington (New Hampshire)
Many recreational activities are offered in this area.

Mystic Seaport (Mystic, Connecticut)
This living history museum includes a colonial village.

Portland Head Light (Portland, Maine)
This landmark includes a museum and park.

World Wide Web

The Fifty States
www.infoplease.com/states.html
This site has a clickable U.S. map that gives facts about each of the 50 states, plus images of each state's flag.

These sites have pictures, statistics, and other facts about each state in New England.

Connecticut
www.kids.state.ct.us

Maine
www.state.me.us/sos/kids

Massachusetts
www.mass-vacation.com

New Hampshire
www.visitnh.gov/forkids.html

Rhode Island
www.visitrhodeisland.com

Vermont
www.vermont.gov/find-facts/kidspage.html

Timeline

A.D. 1000
Viking sailors explore the islands and coast of Maine, and Cape Cod.

1604
Explorer Samuel de Champlain establishes a French settlement in Maine.

1620
The Pilgrims land at Plymouth Rock and establish the Plymouth Colony.

1633
A trading post is built in Connecticut.

1636
Settlers arrive in Rhode Island.

1692
The Salem witch trials are held.

1763
British claim all territory in New England after defeating the French in the French and Indian War.

1770
British soldiers fire on an angry mob in Boston (Boston Massacre).

1772
A British ship is burned by Rhode Island colonists—the first action against English rule.

1773
Patriots dump a shipload of British Tea into Boston Harbor (Boston Tea Party).

1775
The American Revolution begins.

1776
George Washington forces the British out of Boston.

1788
Connecticut, Massachusetts, and New Hampshire become states.

1823
Alexander Twilight becomes the first African-American college graduate in the U.S. at Middlebury College in Vermont.

1826
The first U.S. railroad is built in Quincy, Massachusetts.

1833
The first public library in America is founded in Peterborough, New Hampshire.

1837
Samuel Morse of Massachusetts introduces his dots and dashes system for the electric telegraph.

1853
Franklin Pierce of New Hampshire becomes U.S. President.

1860
Maine's Hannibal Hamlin is named Abraham Lincoln's vice president.

1876
The first telephone is demonstrated in Boston by Alexander Graham Bell.

1881
Chester A. Arthur of Vermont becomes U.S. President.

1898
The first American subway system is opened in Boston.

1900
The first U.S. Navy submarine, Holland, is launched in Connecticut.

1923
Calvin Coolidge of Vermont becomes U.S. President.

1928
The first computer is developed at M.I.T.

1948
Maine's Margaret Chase Smith is the first woman elected to the U.S. Senate.

1954
The first successful kidney transplant is performed in Boston.

1960
John F. Kennedy of Massachusetts is elected president of United States.

1971
The first e-mail is sent in Massachusetts over the ARPANET, an early version of the Internet.

2004
The Boston Red Sox win the World Series.

States at a Glance

Connecticut
Became State: 1788
Nickname: The Constitution State
Motto: He who transplanted still sustains
Capital: Hartford
State Bird: American robin
State Tree: White oak
State Flower: Mountain laurel
State Animal: Sperm whale
State Song: Yankee Doodle

Maine
Became State: 1820
Nickname: The Pine Tree State
Motto: I Lead
Capital: Augusta
State Bird: Chickadee
State Tree: White pine
State Flower: White pine cone and tassel
State Animal: Moose
State Song: State of Maine

Massachusetts
Became State: 1788
Nickname: The Bay State
Motto: By the sword we seek peace, but peace only under liberty
Capital: Boston
State Bird: Chickadee
State Tree: American elm
State Flower: Mayflower
State Animal: None
State Song: All Hail to Massachusetts

New Hampshire
Became State: 1788
Nickname: The Granite State
Motto: Live free or die
Capital: Concord
State Bird: Purple finch
State Tree: White birch
State Flower: Purple lilac
State Animal: White-tailed deer
State Song: Old New Hampshire

Rhode Island
Became State: 1790
Nickname: The Ocean State
Motto: Hope
Capital: Providence
State Bird: Rhode Island red hen
State Tree: Red maple
State Flower: Violet
State Animal: None
State Song: Rhode Island

Vermont
Became State: 1791
Nickname: The Green Mountain State
Motto: Vermont, Freedom and Unity
Capital: Montpelier
State Bird: Hermit thrush
State Tree: Sugar maple
State Flower: Red clover
State Animal: Morgan horse
State Song: These Green Mountains

Glossary

adapted changed or adjusted

ancestors people from whom one is descended

architecture design of houses or buildings

border dividing line between one country or region and another

climate weather conditions of a place

colonist someone who lives in a newly settled area

cog railroad railway used on mountains that has a system in which a special wheel fitted to the train clicks its way along the track

cultures customs, language, art, and ideas shared by groups of people

economy system of money in a place

garnet gemstone that is usually dark red in color

granite common, hard rock often used in buildings

habitat correct place for a person or animal to live

immigrants people who leave their country to settle in another

independence freedom from others

isolated alone or far away from others

landscape land that has beautiful scenery

Latino person whose family comes from Latin America

legislature group of people with the power to make or change laws

mainland main land mass of a country or area

manufacturing turning something into a useful product

megalopolis huge chain of cities that have grown together

metropolitan area region that includes a city and the suburbs around it

migrating moving from one region to another

New World North and South America

nuclear submarine specialized watercraft powered by nuclear energy that operate underwater

population number of people living in a state or region

preserve land kept in its natural state

Quakers religious group whose members try to live simply

resistance group of people who seek independence from another group

seafaring making a living from the ocean

service industry work connected with the serving of customers

sound long, wide inlet or body of water connecting larger bodies of water

subject person under the control or power of another person or group

synagogue Jewish place of worship

telecommunications the science of communicating over long distances

textile cloth that is woven or knitted

tidal affected by waters that periodically rise and fall

Underground Railroad system of places set up by people who helped runaway slaves

Index